Unbelievable Blessings

PERSONAL REFLECTIONS, OBSERVATIONS AND THOUGHTS

BY

WILBUR BROWER

EDITED BY BRIDGETTE BRYANT

OTHER BOOKS BY THE AUTHOR

What a Difference a Comma Makes — the Complete Guide for Understanding and Applying Correctly Punctuation Marks and Symbols Commonly Used In English Grammar (2015)

Seven C's of Success — Developing the Attributes, Attitudes and Behaviors to Achieve All You Want Out of Life (2013)

Defining Your Success — You Decide What You Want Out of Life (2013)

When Justice Calls — A novel (2013)

Traffic Signs on the Road of Life (2012), co-authored with Cynthia Brower

Of Life, Love and Learning — Selected Poems and Educational Raps, Rhythms and Rhymes (2012)

English Grammar and Writing Made Easy — Learn to Communicate More Accurately, Clearly and Concisely (2012)

Personal Care Journal — The Adult Years (2000, co-authored)

A Little Book of Big Principles-Values and Virtues for a More Successful Life (1998 and 2012)

Me Teacher, Me...Please! — Observation about Parents, Students, Teachers and the Teaching-Learning Process (2001)

Visit the Author's Amazon Page:
http://tinyurl.com/ckw5ms8

Copyright © 2016 by Wilbur L. Brower, Ph.D.

Library of Congress Control Number: 2016933793

Brower, Wilbur L.

1. Spirituality
2. Self-help
3. Gratitude

Correspondence to the author should be directed to:

PwP Publishing
P. O. Box 565
Trenton, NC 28585

E-mail: wlbrower@gmail.com

ISBN-13: 978-0-9894838-6-5

GRATITUDE IS NOT ONLY THE GREATEST OF
VIRTUES,
BUT THE PARENT OF ALL OTHERS.

- MARCUS TULLIUS CICERO
(106-43) ROMAN ORATOR

TABLE OF CONTENTS

COUNT YOUR BLESSINGS

When upon life's billows you are tempest tossed,
When you are discouraged, thinking all is lost,
Count your many blessings, name them one by one,
And it will surprise you what the Lord hath done.

Refrain
Count your blessings, name them one by one,
Count your blessings, see what God hath done!
Count your blessings, name them one by one,
And it will surprise you what the Lord hath done.

Are you ever burdened with a load of care?
Does the cross seem heavy you are called to bear?
Count your many blessings, every doubt will fly,
And you will keep singing as the days go by.

Refrain

When you look at others with their lands and gold,
Think that Christ has promised you His wealth untold;
Count your many blessings. Wealth can never buy
Your reward in heaven, nor your home on high.

Refrain

So, amid the conflict whether great or small,
Do not be disheartened, God is over all;
Count your many blessings, angels will attend,
Help and comfort give you to your journey's end.

Refrain

Words: Johnson Oatman, Jr., in *Songs for Young People*,
by Edwin Excell (Chicago, Illinois: 1897).
Music: Edwin O. Excell (MIDI, score).

Introduction

While I was growing up in a small rural community in central North Carolina and attending a Presbyterian Church my forbearers established, the congregation, in a manner unlike anything for which the Presbyterian denomination was known, would often sing a rousing and spirit-filled rendition of *Count Your Blessings*. I always thought about the significance of the words, but the full measure of their meaning did not sink into my spirit and become part of my consciousness until I was well into my adult years. I then learned to find joy and blessing in everything I did, no matter how challenging or mundane, and to see each situation as if it were the most important thing I had ever done. The recognition that everything I had ever encountered could have been a blessing introduced me to the possibility that it probably was exactly what I needed at the time to mold me into the person God wanted me to be. I could no longer see situations as curses or drudgery, but as circumstances that could serve many useful purposes. I never looked at my life the same way.

One of the most humbling and sobering realities I have found is that my mere existence, or the fact that I was born, has absolutely nothing to do with me personally. I owe my existence to those who are responsible for my being: my parents James Wilbur and Resa McGregor. I count all they did for me and taught me as blessings.

I can imagine that there are many who feel that their lives have been so horrific and unfulfilled that they, if they had a choice, would have preferred not having the blessing of life. Think of all the horrible and unimaginable things some people have endured and survived then went on to give the world extraordinary accomplishments.

It is easy to believe that some situations can be disastrous and will doom us for the remainder of our lives. It is hard to believe that these situations were exactly what we needed in our lives at that time to prepare us for other, situations we will encounter later. We just have to look beyond our current circumstances and situations with an attitude and belief that they will pass.

While reading through the text, you will quickly learn that there is little or nothing I have written that is profound or earth-shattering. I offer all of it as personal observations, reflections and thoughts that I've often elected to put forth as assertions. You may disagree with some or all of them, but that is your choice. However, if you find that any sliver of it expands your understanding of your purpose in life, informs your thinking about how you see the world and your place in it, or enriches your relationship with yourself and with others, then this small publication will have been worth the effort. The fact that you have read this far is a blessing, and I encourage you to share any insights and understandings with others, especially those who might not see or understand all of the things which they can and should be thankful for.

CHAPTER ONE

"How did it get so late so soon?
It's night before it's afternoon.
December is here before it's June.
My goodness, how the time has flewn.
How did it get so late so soon?"

-- Dr. Seuss

THE UNBELIEVABLE BLESSING OF TIME

Time is like a person whom you once met and, initially, didn't care for very much. Then you got to know them, how they work, how they think, and how utterly kind and generous they are on the inside even though it's almost impossible to see on the outside. You kept looking and you came to find that this friend, who seemed so elusive, was actually necessary, dependable and very much needed.

The problem we have with time is that we often don't pay too much attention to it until it's doing something that we don't like. Nothing seemed to take as long, no desire seems so gone without, until time points it out to us. The thing is, time is really only allowing us a breather between memorable moments that we combine together and refer to as 'life.' Without the time in between, though it may seem a bit dull, life would be one long rush of ups and downs, without a break. It would just be up one day and, down the next, repetitively. Even though life can sometimes feel like this anyway, that feeling is only a dramatization of our emotional thought when, in reality, there is always transitional time in between. That time allots for healing, reflecting, re-strategizing, and the rebuilding of hope.

That hope is what carries us into the next moment in time, and then it is rekindled yet again, as we go into the next, and rise, and repeat.

LEARNING TO KNOW WHEN YOU ARE STANDING

Time is best looked at in the cumulative way. It is the focus that we give to the unwanted, individual bits that makes the rest of time seem...fuzzy... a blur. What if we were to spend the majority of our time focused upon the times that we've loved the best? It is said that during the best moments, time seems to fly and it does, or at least it seems to, even though it is actually moving at the exact same rate as it was during moments less desired. But what we learn during those moments we carry with us into the next. What nuggets of life and living were gleaned, deposited, and planted down into the knowing of our souls? Could we have really done without the lesson brought to us during that time? Would we really want to?

Understanding the movement of time allows us to have a greater understanding of ourselves. Glimpses from the past, where we have struggled, placed in contrast to visions of better days, gives us a foundation upon which to stand in the knowing of who we are today. Without those moments of contrast, how will we be able to tell how far we have come? More importantly, how would we be able to have the confidence that we could change our today without the proof of having changed our yesterday?

A part of recognizing the impact that the passing minutes, hours, and days has upon our state of mind and, thus, our state of being is the ability to calculate just how much we are capable of, which gives us the energy it takes to do even more. The contrast of the experiences that time ushers in allows us to paint a beautiful canvas of events that ultimately serve as a guide post for who we have become. This gives us the power to select and choose and use these woven events to create the vision of our next reality. It gives us the processing time required in order to receive the clarity that allows us to know that we have the ability to take our allotted time into our own hands and mold it to help us become whatsoever we see fit.

In all our deeds, the proper value and respect for time determines success or failure.

- Malcolm X

LEARNING HOW TO USE TIME

Time is the most consistent and dependable partner you will ever meet in your entire life, and furthermore, it does not discriminate! It doesn't care what race you are, what kind of day you had, how much money you have in the bank, or any other demographic characteristic by which humans tend to compare others to themselves. Time is interested solely upon one topic: progress. And you may do best to join it in this endeavor.

We all have been blessed with twenty-four hours each day, but we often do not instinctively know what to do with it, and we often do not know that the ability to learn how to use it is available. This is not a topic that is taught in schools or passed down in most family lineage, but the ability to master the use of your time is wisdom that will benefit you all the days of your life. It can be the distinguishing factor between a life fully lived or one looked back upon in regret.

We all have a limited amount of time on earth and we will eventually expend that time, whether we use it to the fullest extent possible or choose otherwise. When it's gone, it's gone; we don't get more. We cannot barter, borrow or buy it, no matter how clever, persuasive, or rich we happen to be. So when we wake in the morning with a brand new slate of opportunity and potential, consider making the choice to set your mind for greatness. Make the decision that, from now on, you will use your time to the greatest benefit of, first, yourself and then of others. Use these affirmations to help you create new habits that will position you to be able to receive the blessings of time:

"Today, I Will Use This Time To Be Truly Who I Am."
Just as there is only a limited amount of time, there is also only a limited amount of you. One, to be exact. You are an original, fabulous creation and nothing on this planet is a duplicate of you. Therefore, when you rise and go out into the world, you are forced to take yourself with you, but it is a choice to let yourself be truly seen by others. You do this by removing the masks of guilt and fear and opening yourself up to potential judgment, becoming vulnerable to all the environmental and social factors that surround you. This may sound like a scary thing to do, and it may very well be, but it is also the only way to truly be alive. Freeing your mind of caring what other people think (or at least making the decision to ignore what they think) will open up your life's experiences like nothing else. Your vibrancy, your passion, your internal greatness

will be allowed to come out and fly around in the fullest of its creativity. So the next time you go outside of your doors, go out as the beautiful dance of light and power that you are.

"Today, I Will Do My Best Using My Time Wisely."
When you do your very best, it doesn't mean that you necessarily will achieve any sort of stated objective. It simply means that you show up and do whatever you can do to the very best of your ability. The purpose of this is internal fulfillment, a personal satisfaction of accomplishment. When you do something and you know you've done the very best that you can do, even if you don't get the results you were aiming for, you will know inside that you did the best you could and, therefore, you will still feel empowered and strong. Those feelings will enable you to readjust your strategy and increase your probability of success the next time around.

> Time is the coin of your life. It is the only coin you have,
> and only you can determine how it will be spent.
> Be careful lest you let other people spend it for you.
>
> - Carl Sandburg

"Today Is a New Day; I Will Seize Every Moment of It."
It is easy to put off until tomorrow things that we want to do today, but we all know how that saying goes. I have attempted to capture the essence of this

thinking in the book titled *Of Life, Love and Learning-Selected Poems and Educational Raps, Rhythms and Rhymes* (2012):

> It's only this moment that's promised.
> All past moments were guaranteed.
> All future moments are wishful,
> So, this is the moment to seize.

It is easy to saunter through life believing that we have more time remaining than we actually do. There is no digital countdown timer or clock telling us that the end of our allotted time is near (and thank goodness for that). Since we don't know how long we really have, the only option is to maximize each and every day. Social expectations and responsibilities sometimes seem to get in the way of our ability to fill each day with doing what we truly want to do, but this is only an illusion. We are fully in control of how we spend each and every one of the 24 hours we have in each day. It is up to us how we spend them, and only fear can keep us from making them great. So in the morning when we rise, try doing something different if we desire to yield a different result. We can say to ourselves, "Today, I will shed my fears and seize every opportunity available to me."

THE UNBELIEVABLE BLESSING OF TIME

I am very blessed that I was able to gain the knowledge and wisdom required to understand the value of time and make the decision to use wisely all I have been allotted. I realized early on that I could not manage time; I could only manage myself during the days that I call mine. In that learning, I have become blessed by time and no longer curse it or consider it my enemy. Instead, I work with it like a faithful partner, riding the waves of its peaks and valleys and painting a beautiful picture that I will one day hang on a wall, step back, and be proud to have created.

QUESTIONS TO THINK ABOUT....

1. What have you done with your blessing of time?

2. What do you have to show for the blessing of time you have been granted?

3. Are you using your time to entertain or to educate yourself?

4. Have you used any of your time to help others?

CHAPTER TWO

Religious Freedom

"I never will, by any word or act, bow to the shrine of intolerance, or admit a right of inquiry into the religious opinions of others."

-- Thomas Jefferson, letter to Edward Dowse, April 19, 1803

THE UNBELIEVABLE BLESSING OF RELIGIOUS FREEDOM

The vision of the United States of America is that every individual be granted the freedoms of life, liberty, and the pursuit of happiness. Encompassed in that vision is the freedom and choice of religion. Given this guiding, fundamental freedom, which grants the privilege of selecting your own state of being, it is no wonder that the United States is still considered one of the greatest countries of the world.

The ability to define and practice the religion of one's choice (which includes choosing to have no religion at all) is one of the most controversial conversations among societies today, and it always has been. Freedom of Religion truly is the ability to choose one's own basis for existence. This is so because the choice of religion is really just a way of defining one's morals and one's general expectations for the flow of life (and for the hereafter). Therefore, this freedom is not one that can really be looked at as being optional. To not have this freedom would be a complete injustice to the individual, for he would not be allowed to follow his own mind. Being cut off from that internal guidance when making a decision would ultimately be a detriment to his community and to society as a whole. It may even be to the detriment of the entire world because that individual would be cut off from being who he or she really is and, therefore, would have nothing to contribute to the whole.

> Religious freedom is a fundamental right which shapes the way we interact socially and personally with our neighbors whose religious views differ from our own.
> - Pope Francis

INDICATORS OF A LACK OF RELIGIOUS FREEDOM

The International Religious Freedom (IRF) Act defines five violations of religious freedom. These occur when an individual, organization, or government places arbitrary prohibitions upon, restrictions of, or punishment for: (i) assembling for peaceful religious activities such as worship, preaching, and prayer, including arbitrary registration requirements; (ii) speaking freely about one's religious beliefs; (iii) changing one's religious beliefs and affiliation; (iv) possessing and distributing religious literature, including Bibles and other sacred texts; (v) raising one's children in the religious teachings and practices of one's choice.

When reviewing a country's state of religious freedom, laws and policies of concern are those who:

- Restrict the right to hold a religious belief;
- Limit the right to change religious belief;
- Restrict the freedom to have an allegiance to a religious leader;
- Disparage individuals or groups on the basis of their religion;
- Discriminate against religious persons in education, the military, employment opportunities or in health services;
- Require the designation of religion on passports or national identity documents, either overtly or in code;
- Restrict religious assembly;
- Restrict religious expression.

According to the IRF Act (Section 402), a country is designated by the Department of State as a Country of Particular Concern (CPC) if its government is determined to have engaged in or tolerated particularly severe violations of religious freedom. The IRF Act defines particularly severe violations of religious freedom as systematic, ongoing, egregious violations. These include torture, and humane cruelty, and any other flagrant denial of the right to life committee or security. [1]

Civil rights laws and regulations such as these are considered by some to be the highest calling of government. They are to protect the inalienable rights of human beings and set a standard for behavioral expectations around the world. This is the foundation of civilization.

"Everyone shall have the right to freedom of thought, conscience, and religion. This right shall include freedom to have or to adopt a religion or belief of his choice, and freedom, either individually or in community with others and in public or private, to manifest his religion or belief in worship, observance, practice, and teaching"
- Article 18(1) of the International Covenant on Civil and Political Rights

THE SEPARATION OF CHURCH AND STATE

Government and religion have been deemed to remain as separate bodies for good reason. The term "freedom of religion" implies that, in your personal life, one is free to practice whatever religion he or she desires. So, as an American, if a person wants to be Buddhist, Christian, Hindu, Muslim, or follow no religion at all, that person is free to do so. This is a much-needed and well-to-be-praised protection of a freedom. In its fullness, this protection provides for a change of heart as well. One may choose to give "sun salutations" this week and "speak in tongues" the next. This is the fullness of religious freedom.

Americans have the freedom to practice their religion during every waking hour that they decide. They can do so publicly, in religious places of worship, or privately within their own homes. They can even take a sabbatical and skip church for several weeks. They have the freedom to decide.

The problem that often occurs is when others attempt to force their personal religious beliefs upon people who have different beliefs. Unfortunately, government policies cannot protect us from experiencing social and religious discrimination. However, governments can make an effort to ensure that policies and laws restricting individual choices and freedoms are not implemented. In establishing laws and regulations that prohibit a person's ability to make decisions that do not conflict with their own individual beliefs in support of decisions that coincide with other religious beliefs, there is a conflict of freedom. By making laws that support the belief of one religion and overriding the beliefs of other individuals, Government is actually enforcing the opposite of freedom of religion. Any law based on religious beliefs and any law that restricts an individual from making a decision that is in-line with their own beliefs is a violation of the First Amendment. [2]

Blind faith in belief-system, ideologies, doctrine or dogma can never set us free. Only the knowledge of truth can liberate us from the slavery of doctrine, dogmas, blind faiths and religious sects.
- Banani Ray [3]

THE FULLNESS OF LIFE BROUGHT BY RELIGIOUS FREEDOM

Truly having the freedom of religion is like living in a world entirely open to you with no boundaries or limitations. The only boundaries therein are the ones that you create for yourself. And in creating them, you do so with a specific purpose in mind; one that comes from within, one that defines who you are, what you believe to be true, and entirely supports your reason for existence.

When one is allowed to make choices from this state of balance and understanding, decisions take on a more culpable meaning. It would not be a stretch to say that, since we are all, technically, one body working together to populate the earth, regardless of what our religious beliefs are, the ability to have the freedom to make decisions regarding the actions one will take in their life is more beneficial to the whole because it comes from within that person's heart, a heart that beats with the same desires every human being on the planet has. No matter what our personal ambitions, we are all seeking love, comfort, and security. If each person were to abandon the decision to do things for fear-based reasons and instead make their decisions based on internal instincts, it is unimaginable how amazing the result would be and how quickly our world changes to reflect the benefit of acting upon one's inner knowing.

In order to create this beautiful vision, we must not only have the religious freedoms granted by government, but we must also grant religious freedoms to ourselves. The freedom to make choices that perhaps do not make sense...the freedom to explore things that are new and uncharted...the freedom to choose one's own career path...the freedom to be an individual without receiving judgment or guilt from others who have a different belief. Having religious freedoms gives us the creative mindset to come up with these ideas, but the limitations on freedom that we place upon one another through judgment and ridicule keep us from living this vision of utopia.

THE UNBELIEVABLE BLESSING OF RELIGIOUS FREEDOM

I grew up Presbyterian, a religious belief some ridicule and find alien because of the subdued nature of its worship ceremonies and rituals. But as a Presbyterian, I learned to treat all people with dignity and respect, even when they did not reciprocate. I was raised on the philosophy to always help your neighbor, be full of honesty and integrity, always keep your word, and work hard to accomplish things you set out to. I was raised to always look for the good in others, even when they have demonstrated something quite different. The unbelievable blessing that I received from having the freedom to practice this religion, despite the unfavorable opinion of others, is that it was inclusive and affirming. It sustained me during times of challenge and uncertainty, and it propelled me toward personal goals that conventional wisdom said were unattainable. And it is a blessing that has served me well and allowed me to become the man I am today.

1.   What are your religious beliefs, if you have any?

2.   Are those beliefs working for you or against you?

3.   Are your religious beliefs affirming life for all or destroying the lives of others because they have different beliefs?

4.   What perceptions do you have of religions that are different from yours?

5.   Do you *know* the perceptions to be true, or are they things that you've always *thought*, *heard*, or *believed*?

6.   How are others' religious beliefs really different from yours?

CHAPTER THREE

Family

"Having somewhere to go is home. Having someone to love is family. Having both is a blessing. The love of a family is life's greatest blessings. In time of test, family is best."

-- **Burmese Proverb**

THE UNBELIEVABLE BLESSING OF FAMILY

The blessing of family is in knowing that you are never ever alone.

Family by no means requires a blood relation; some of our greatest allies and closest kin can come from our friends, peers, and even from perfect strangers. The highest benefit of the family blessing comes in knowing and having the ability to witness the fact that we are all connected and related in some form or fashion even with or without the molecular connection. These ties that bind, if they are truly accepted within the heart, can open up the door to a freedom in life that nothing else can replicate. The liberty is in knowing that no matter where you go or what you do, there will always be someone to catch you if you fall. The safety net is a tremendous blessing and can provide the freedom and the wings required for an individual to set their destination and take flight.

DEFINING FAMILY: A UNIT OR A MINDSET?

A family unit can be described as people born into the same bloodline who do not necessarily live together but who share a common bond in genetics.

In days of old, extended family members would live together for decades. This is a great contrast to our current societal norms in which children are expected to move out of the home around the age of 18, typically never to return to until their mid-30s. Although said in jest, some *thirty-somethings* are, in fact, finding themselves returning to the homestead these days due to economic struggles. This highlights one of the beautiful blessings of family: the ability to have someone to lean upon. Although crucial to long-term success, having someone to lean on, if taken to the extreme, can also become a hindrance. Human beings are sometimes more effective under pressure and when their backs are against a wall; therefore, having a safety net can sometimes lessen tenacity. It is, however, a balancing act, because not having the safety net at all can cause a person to experience feelings of debilitation when faced with a challenging task and, thereafter, be unable to move forward due to feelings of hopelessness or fear.

If family is viewed as a mindset, as opposed to being just a structural makeup, the thoughts of the person experiencing that mindset would be inclusive and full of optimism. They would approach life with a sort of knowing and a deep understanding that everything in the earth is there to support their personal endeavors, and this type of excitement would yield a level of freedom that would open them up to a world of infinite possibilities.

In this mindset, the person would consider a grocery store clerk to be their cousin; the bank teller to be a close friend; and the secretary to be like a long-lost sister. Every person and everything encountered would be viewed as having a family connection. The family mindset can bring a person to a place where they experience more hope and excitement in everyday living; they would have a happier life, filled with positive experiences and unshakable faith.

"You don't choose your family.
They are God's gift to you, as you are to them."
- Bishop Desmond Tutu

CHOOSING WHO'S WHO

It is true that family does not necessarily mean related by blood. In fact, those who do not have a strong support system of family members often fill that gap with close, personal relationships with friends who feel "closer than a brother."

Many people feel that these relationships are even more valuable than relationships we are born into because there are less preconceived notions and expectations. Friends tend to be less attached to the idea of trying to get another to behave in a certain way or to do a certain thing. This type of "family" can provide the best of both worlds since the individual is more free to be themselves and is, therefore, more confident, and able to take risks while simultaneously having a safety net of companions to lean upon for support.

It can also be said that there is something to the fact that we are able to voluntarily choose the friends whom we claim as family; but, in contrast, it is possible that those whom we decide to hold near and dear are just as naturally selected as family members. This is because we typically attract to ourselves others who are like us and who have similar ideals. When presented with the opportunity to create a new friendship, unlike in family ties, we can choose to say yay or nay, but if we pass on the opportunity, the next potential friend will be very similar in design unless there has been a great change or shift which occurred within ourselves.

Not only do we attract individuals who are like us into our lives, but we also attract circumstances and situations into our lives that mimic and support our frame of mind, be they positive or negative. Recalling this natural law of nature can be very useful in all of our dealings and can help us build more joyful, desired associations and more long-lasting friendships.

THE BLESSING AS A CURSE

A very humbling and sobering reality is that we have no choice about the blood family into which we are born or in which we often find ourselves. With few exceptions, we have little or nothing to do or say about the matter. Family, however it is constructed or has evolved, can be a complicated social unit that has the potential to be either a blessing or a curse; and, sometimes, simultaneously both! Family has the capacity to bring us unspeakable happiness as well as profound sadness and sorrow.

Unfortunately, some families exist in name only. Poet Robert Frost said, "Home is the place where, when you have to go there, they have to take you in." In this regard, for some families, it is possible to be physically with family members and still not feel at home. For this reason, at times, a more independent relationship from the family can create a much more positive atmosphere for spiritual and emotional development. Family can sometimes interfere with our ability to see beyond current circumstances, and can even prohibit us from seeing and truly engaging with the person we have grown into becoming over the years. It is often difficult for family to see a person as anything other than the child they always thought they knew.

Comedian George Burns famously said, "Happiness is having a large, loving, caring, close- knit family…in another city." He's not alone in that sentiment; sometimes family is best appreciated and cherished from a distance.

CREATING BOUNDARIES TO BALANCE THE FAMILY DYNAMIC

It is important to always remember the value of keeping your own heart first. This is because, with the blessing of family, there is also a sense of responsibility. This responsibility can sometimes lead us to make decisions that we would not otherwise make. The importance of staying true to oneself must override the temptation to please others. If not, eventually we may find ourselves looking back not only with regret and remorse, but also with bitterness toward the loved ones we were trying to please.

THE UNBELIEVABLE BLESSING OF FAMILY

It is vital to remember that one must always maintain their own mind without regard to the judgment of others. In doing so, you are able to stay true to yourself, and stay on the journey that has been purposed within your heart. There can be no joy found in taking a step off that path and, no matter what your loved one may say to you, they would never truly wish you to do so. When a loved one opposes the plan or vision of another, it is usually out of fear of the outcome. They don't want to see their precious, close family-member hurt and, therefore, act in ways they think will be protective for them. Though it is kind and considerate, if it goes against the internal dialogue of the person who is trying to follow their heart, it will hurt them more than help. This is why it is very crucial to allow others the freedom to make their own decisions and be whomsoever they want to be. Though loving one another is vital to our advancement, loving oneself must always come first in order to obtain the greater good for all.

It is up to you to establish a relationship with family in a way that it will not prohibit you from achieving your full potential. In my own life, I could not always look to family for financial support, but I could always feel my family's moral support and belief in my ability to succeed. With experience, one learns that a reconfiguration of relationships with your family is the best way to endure many of the stresses and strains that can occur. With an end-result approach to dealing with family matters, one cannot help but find peace and balance in whichever path you choose.

QUESTIONS TO THINK ABOUT....

1. Have you felt your family being a positive influence in your journey to obtain your dreams and goals?

2. Are you allowing emotional feelings toward your family members to keep you from dealing with them in a healthy way?

3. Do you avoid communicating with your family in order to keep the peace at the expense of your own self-empowerment?

4. Have you shown your family how much you love them and appreciate them for supporting your success?

CHAPTER FOUR

Good
Health

"The greatest wealth, is health"

-- Unknown

THE UNBELIEVABLE
BLESSING OF GOOD HEALTH

The blessing of good health is like having the keys to a castle while also being the king or queen of it. No matter what goodness a person may procure on this earth, whether it be a good job, great wealth, or fairytale-like romance, good health is required to receive the full enjoyment of all circumstances. Without it, even the best of times can seem like the worst of times. So we respect and honor the blessing of good health and welcome it with open arms into the experience of our everyday life.

MINDING WHAT WE PUT IN THE BODY

Some years ago, there was a sudden health craze and food content fad in the mainstream media that spotlighted ingredient panels on the sides of boxes and packaging. Gurus and fitness experts from all around the country were stepping forward to put in their two-cents worth and tell the world about their amazing miracle weight-loss cure, new special juice diet, guaranteed effective workout regime, or whatever else they had decided to present as the ultimate solution to America's perceived problem of physical dissatisfaction.

While some of these ideas, plans, and gimmicks did carry an underlying positive message and helpful information, most of them were covered in sales tactics, and many were not taken seriously because they were much too focused on a quick-fix solution to something that required more of a lifestyle change.

Achieving relatively good health, in fact, is a rather simple process. The body is a machine which works perfectly in its own capacity, as long as it is well-fed and well-maintained. Each body is different in some ways, and, therefore, each individual must determine what the definition of personal welfare is for him or herself. However, in general, we all know that healthy foods typically tend to be those that grow in some way from the earth. We can also agree that exercise in any form best suited for each individual is a very helpful method in maintaining an active energy level.

The majority of success in physical health endeavors is found when the person is taking action with the goal of simply feeling better. Weight loss pills, diet fads, and the desire to look different for a particular event or person simply is not enough motivation to create a consistently healthy lifestyle and, therefore, it is best to opt for making a decision to just do whatever it takes for your body to feel healthy and vibrant on a day-to-day basis. The rest will take care of itself.

"There's nothing more important than our good health - that's our principal capital asset."
- Arlen Specter (U. S, Congress 1979-2012)

GOOD HEALTH IS MORE THAN PHYSICAL

As important as it is to have a healthy body with optimally functioning parts and internal organs, good health doesn't stop there. Good health includes the state in which one's mind operates. It is said that as a man thinks so he is, and, therefore, it may be accurate to deduce that the health of the mind may even supersede that of the body. If one runs into conflict in the body, and that man is however he thinks, then won't the mind have the potential to override the body?

Poor mental health can be identified as being extremely deficient in cases of paranoia, lack of empathy, or in having an attitude of lack in which one tends to find fault in everything, never seeing the glass as half full.

The process of getting to a healthy mind involves clearing out the thoughts that do not serve any longer. Psychologically, our minds are programmed to protect us from harm. Therefore, we often, ironically, hold on to negative memories in an attempt to prevent the recurrence of that circumstance. As some of these steady reminders are very valuable, others can prove to be quite detrimental when the time has come to begin to think in a new way.

The fear of being hurt in love is a good example of a protective idea that must be overridden. Almost all of us have experienced it, and we tend to have the exact same resolution: never fall in love again. Not only is this an impractical answer, but it is also not true to our hearts. We are born with the capability to give, produce, and accept love into our lives; and it fills our spirit in many ways. Regardless of how much we have been hurt by past relationships, we need love and it is crucial in order for us to carry on. If we think back to the very first love that captivated our soul and then tore us apart on the inside, had we previously had the experience of falling in love and getting hurt, and, from that, made the decision to never love again prior to that wonderful first love, then we never would have experienced that relationship. This is what we do to ourselves every time we enter into the arena of potential new romance holding up a wall built by a previous experience of pain. To experience the bliss, we have to let go of the past and clear our minds of any unhelpful memories.

The mind stores that memory in an attempt to keep us safe and secure. Although it may have been useful while recovering from the painful relationship so there was enough time to heal, the need for protection no longer applies and must be removed in order for there to be new opportunities for the person to embrace love again as if it were the very first time. The need to remove protective thoughts that are no longer serving is just another way of letting go of fears. Take an inventory of the thoughts that guide and dictate your decisions and actions, get rid of them, and allow new experiences to come in and paint a different picture. Then you'll find yourself on the road to good mental health which, again, is the foundation of good physical health.

"Diseases of the soul are more dangerous
and more numerous than those of the body."

- Cicero

THE EMOTIONS OF GOOD HEALTH

Feeling healthy is an emotional state of being. Coupled with the health of the body and the clearness of the mind, the experience of having emotional health can lead a person to the best life they've ever lived.

Although they are entirely invisible, emotions tend to rule life more than anything else. We can know with our minds that we should make a certain decision; there can be physical circumstances which make that same choice stand out. Sometimes, despite all of the evidence, we choose to ignore our physical senses and follow the musings of the heart. This, then, means that in spite of what we see and what we know to be true, our emotions override our logic and, thus, emotional stability is crucial to our long-term happiness and success.

Obtaining emotional health primarily involves only one thing: keeping yourself happy by doing what you truly want to do. This includes short-term, long-run, and everything in between. From big dreams to fleeting and random thoughts, showing love for self by honoring internal desires makes the soul shine brighter than anything else in the world. By giving yourself the gift of self-fulfillment, you're positioned for emotional health, and can give those around you the opportunity to benefit from your mindset.

GOOD HEALTH IS THE START OF A GREAT LIFE

Imagine operating on all three cylinders and you will be imagining the most fulfilled life a person can experience:

1) To have physical health in the body where everything works at its peak, and moves freely and comfortably;

2) To have mental health in the freedom of the mind, giving the ability to allow new experiences and be positively impacted by others; and

3) To have true freedom from the judgment of self, applied by the open acceptance of all things desired.

This is a life highly lived and overflowing with love and abundance.

"Good health and good sense are two great blessings."
- Latin Proverb

THE UNBELIEVABLE BLESSING OF GOOD HEALTH

It is too easy to take good health for granted, especially if you have been blessed to have it. I have never ingested any substances that are known to destroy or suspected of destroying my body. I've never taken an illegal drug or seriously smoked any tobacco products. Admittedly, I walked around campus a few days during my freshman year in college and puffed on a pipe. That was the "in" thing for me to try until I developed one of the worst sore throats I ever had. This told me, in no uncertain terms, that smoking and tobacco were not for me. I quickly gave up that experiment and never touched a tobacco product again. There was something inside of me that instinctively knew the Blessing of good health took precedent over looking cool and doing what was "in," or the popular thing to do. The gift of having my wisdom, or self-knowing, has certainly served me well.

QUESTIONS TO THINK ABOUT....

1. What am I doing that may be yielding a negative response from my system?

2. What changes can I make to produce a more chemically balanced internal environment?

3. What sacrifices to health have I made in the name of generating more money?

CHAPTER FIVE

Single Parenting

"There are only two lasting bequests we can hope to give our children. One of these is roots, the other, wings."

-- Johann Wolfgang von Goethe

THE UNBELIEVABLE BLESSING OF SINGLE PARENTING

Single parenting, whether as a conscious decision, the result of life's circumstances, or even a series of unintended consequences, can be a blessing. It is amazing how something slightly frowned upon by society can actually be greatly beneficial if it is contemplated in its proper context. The blessing of single parenting can be found in the actions. Children are often casualties of the decisions made by their parents, which should never be the case, but all too often, many of them do. In those cases, it is the responsibility of the parents to make better choices and do what is necessary to create a healthy and balanced environment for the children. In the case of single parenting, the duties are the same, the resources can be quite different, but the results are well worth the effort.

As a single parent, the first challenge is in getting over the mental roadblocks that one can set up. Once accomplished, the way is paved for the opportunity to share with the child direct, one-on-one, powerful lessons and encouraging examples of how to be a phenomenal human being and grow to have an outstanding life. There is no substitute for the ability to focus solely upon one person and glean wisdom from that engagement; this benefit goes both ways, for the parent and the child.

"Everything depends on upbringing."
- Leo Tolstoy's *War and Peace*

The blessing of being a single parent typically turns out to be more of a life-changing event for the parent than for the child; in a positive way. Being in a position where one must always put their best foot forward, because they are being not only closely watched, but often mimicked can apply more than just a little bit of pressure to succeed. This pressure can, however, be overridden by the power of love and by the desire to show someone so important how to have a better life. Once the fear of failure is gone and the pressure has been dealt with, a gorgeous type of dance begins to occur.

In the dance, the musical notes are the words and actions of the single parent; they become movement and motions brought on by the beat of the thoughts the parent wishes to cultivate in the mind of the child; thoughts that he or she will use to make decisions in life that will shape the entirety of their days. The beat of the song provides a chorus for life;

a deeply-planted flow and rhythm to follow. This music dictates how the child will choose to conduct him or her-self; it helps define who they will become.

A blessing of single parenting can be found in the fact that it is much easier to create a focused rhythm within which the child can grow into a balanced and emotionally well-adjusted human being.

OVERCOMING THE STIGMA

As with any type of conformed judgment or stereotype, the stigma attached to being a single parent is one that must be overcome by the person experiencing it. Stigmas primarily surface due to ignorance of the topic at hand or to falsely perceived notions regarding the topic. Although two-parent homes may have some benefits, those benefits do not make them superior to single-parent homes.

As in all things, something done well by one is not necessarily done well by all; and the performance of one individual, firmly rooted in their own strength and power can outshine the efforts of several individuals who do not have a strong sense of character. It's all about who you are, how you see yourself (or were taught to see yourself), and how you have decided to enrich the world.

In order to overcome the stigma of being a single parent, one must first recognize that if any person who is opposed to their situation knew the background story of the situation, they most likely would have made the exact same decision. We only tend to judge others when we fail to put ourselves in their shoes. Since at the root of human nature we all want the same things, it is a fair assessment that, given the exact same circumstances, we would all make the same choices in our attempt to create the lives we desire. No matter what, people always make the best decisions they possibly can with the information they have available, modified by the conditioning of their minds.

In overcoming the social stigma of single-parenting, it is helpful to decide to disconnect from the awareness of what other people think. Or, at the very least, make an effort to disallow the thoughts of others to affect the decisions that one makes, and the way a person sees himself. If no one ever said or implied that being a single parent was something undesirable, the person who is a single parent would not harbor guilt or negative feelings about the situation. Therefore, it is the awareness of the opinion of others that prevents us from releasing the feelings holding us back, and jumping into the potential power of maintaining a single parent household. In walking away from the opinions of others, a person is able to break free of the binds that come along with the stigma, and embrace where they are in life and do what they would naturally do if free from the judgment of others. They are free to do their very best to make life more enjoyable for themselves and for others; and, in doing so, they will be able to raise a phenomenal new addition to society.

"Children are educated by what the grown-up is
and not by his talk."
- Carl Jung

PUTTING OUR FOCUS WHERE IT BELONGS

Instead of contemplating what others think about us, it is so much more productive and valuable to put our attention toward creating the life, experiences, and memories we truly desire. When we shift our focus, we shift the happenings of our lives to revolve around that thing we are focused upon. In order to fully receive the blessing of single parenting, it is imperative to stay focused on the life that one wants and share vision with their child(ren).

In doing so, they will not only strengthen their ability to create that desired life, but they will also be serving as an example to their child(ren) of how to live their dreams.

NOTWITHSTANDING THE VILLAGE

Just because a person is a single parent does not mean that they must parent alone. In addition to family and friends providing support, there are also several organizations which exist solely to help make the lives of single parents be more enjoyable, functional, and full of growth and stability.

Groups such as the Boys and Girls Club, Big Brothers & Big Sisters of America, Scouting Associations, the YMCA, as well as privately-held and segment-focused nonprofit organizations are available and ready to become a part of the village that raises your child whenever you require it.

"Your children are not your children.
They are sons and daughters of Life's longing for itself.
They come through you but not from you.
And though they are with you yet they belong not to you."
- Kahlil Gibran, Lebanese-American artist, poet, writer
and author of *The Prophet*

THE UNBELIEVABLE BLESSING OF SINGLE PARENTING

I became a single parent when my son was four years old. I am blessed to have had the opportunity to develop a special bond with him that has lasted for more than forty years. It was probably normal to feel deep resentment initially because we were abandoned suddenly, yet not unexpectedly, but it was something that undoubtedly has made both of us stronger.

I essentially placed many dimensions of my life on hold as I was taking care of him, and I learned how to recalibrate my emotional life to optimize the environment for each of us to thrive and survive. I did everything I could to make sure he was as well-adjusted as possible, given our circumstances. I ensured that he received the best dental and medical attention and was always well-kempt. I always made sure he was able to spend time with his mother when he wanted to, and that she was able to spend time with him, even if it inconvenienced me.

We always had kids from the neighborhood coming over to visit and eventually asking if they could become "my child," or if they could live with us. In this atmosphere of sole focus, I was able to develop the art of listening to them and understanding the world from their perspective. I learned their language and lingo and what they valued. All of this helped me to develop a knack of working with children that has been a blessing to me for many years since.

QUESTIONS TO THINK ABOUT....

1. If you are a single parent, how do you approach that responsibility: as a difficult chore or as a golden opportunity?

2. Are you taking advantage of the opportunity to show that you can be the best parent ever?

3. Are you seizing the opportunity to instill values that can endure the turbulent teenage years and overpower the strains and stresses of adulthood?

CHAPTER SIX

Struggle

"Every struggle in your life has shaped you into the person you are today. Be thankful for the hard times, they can only make you stronger.

-- Unknown

THE UNBELIEVABLE BLESSING OF STRUGGLE

It seems as though it would be a great contradiction to consider that struggle could ever be a blessing. However, we all know from life experience that, once the struggle has passed, if we look back with an open heart, we will see that within it were many blessings.

> "It is from our greatest challenges
> that we often discover our true strengths."
> - Wilbur L. Brower
> (from *A Little Book of Big Principles: Values and Virtues for a More Successful Life*)

FINDING OUT WHO YOU REALLY ARE

Struggles happen at different points in each and every journey. It is when one comes out from the struggle that they are able to process it and find what golden nuggets were left behind, sifted from the dirt and rocks. Those nuggets typically turn into the foundation for the next, more advanced challenges and arduous journeys of our lives.

This question is mildly debated, yet the consensus leans towards a "yes." Biologically, even the elements of the earth struggle to evolve and adapt in order to survive in new environments, and thrive on into the next. Once the adaptation occurs, life grows and expands in uncountable quantity, quality, and glorious variation. If we apply the same process of the evolution of biology to the evolution of our individual life experiences, we would determine that, although struggle may occur, when the struggles cease, fields of opportunity for abundance and unmeasurable growth are left in its stead. We find that the struggle was merely a visible indication of a time of elemental change occurring within.

Therefore, if we look at struggle from a more open perspective, it becomes less a focus for pain and more a simple part of the process of living a consistently improving life. When we allow the struggle to simply be a step in a process as opposed to treating it as though it is the fullness of life, we are able to clearly see its blessing and value.

"There's no worse struggle than one that never begins."
- Mexican Proverb

STRUGGLE IS AN OPPORTUNITY

In this more positive light, struggle becomes the evidence of advancement and change. It becomes the required first step for all our greatest successes. As human beings, we often run into complications of resistance when it is time for change. We tend to not embrace change and even fear or run from it. But that is not natural. The very nature of who we are and our physical composition vitally depend upon the inevitability of change. From the moment of conception, to when the fetus grows and evolves into a living, breathing child, change is constantly occurring. The child grows up to become the mother, and, in conceiving and giving birth to the new child, another life inches into our world and helps to continue the momentum of human progress. Change is who we are, and we all participate in its never-ending process whether we want to or not.

REDEFINING THE MEANING OF STRUGGLE

When the concept of struggle begins to transform, the need for replacing the word with something more accurate and definitive becomes apparent. The word "struggle" has become so intertwined with negativity that, when used, it typically communicates meanings of battle, hard times, and painful toil. A more true-to-life conveyance would be to equate the word with simply meaning to show effort or exertion; in other words, the work required to get from here, to there. If it were looked at in this manner, we would more easily be able to digest the idea that struggle is a blessing and, in doing so, more greatly benefit from its presence. We would also advance through its cycles more efficiently.

THERE IS NO LONGER A NEED FOR STRUGGLE

With the knowledge that effort is required for advancement and the wisdom of understanding the blessing of time's consistent promise to always end one situation and begin another, we are able to transcend traditional thoughts of struggle and embrace its powerful aftermath.

Knowing that the situation has come only to bring about the evolution of a more positive and secure existence is a stabilizing truth that allows for the release of resistance and opens the door for a more positive transition. If we are able to finally embrace change as being good, the evident adjustments in life would seem to take a shorter amount of time to get through, and we would appreciate the experience, rather than abhor it. We would benefit from being able to simply allow change to run its course. In doing so, we would become a cooperative organism in the evolution of our lives and feel more peaceful and celebratory about the advances we make.

THE UNBELIEVABLE BLESSING OF STRUGGLE

I have been on my own since three days out of high school, which is more than fifty years. It was up to me to figure out what I would do with my life. I decided rather late that I would go college, and it was up to me to figure out how to pay for it. Some summers I had to work two jobs to get enough money to enroll in the fall semester, and I worked every semester while I was in college.

I was not the most prepared student in college, having come from a small, segregated rural high school. My high school had tattered and torn textbooks, insufficient pieces of Science Lab equipment, and rickety school buses. I also had extenuating circumstances at home that included my having to do morning and after-school farm chores. Because of all my responsibilities, there was never enough time to study and prepare for school as much as I wanted to, so I had to work and study very hard to make up for the areas where I was lacking.

When I arrived at college, I had the mindset that there was no time for playing around - I had to finish this in four years. My determination and effort served me well, as I was on the Dean's List for five semesters out of the eight when I was in college. Those four years gave me the foundation I needed to go on to graduate school and beyond. I learned how to economize my time and optimize my efforts. I learned to read efficiently and effectively, and I learned to write well. I learned the value of resilience and persistence. I also learned the value of strategic thinking and tactical implementation.

The unbelievable blessing of struggle can be found in the gathering of dust that it leaves behind. During the struggles, I learned coping strategies that served me well while I was in the Air Force, an executive with Bell Laboratories/AT&T, and when I was self-employed as a management consultant and trainer. Struggle taught me to become more adaptive contemplative and thoughtful rather than reactionary in times of crises in order to produce a better result. Over the years, the greatest thing I have learned is that effective collaboration with others will always make the struggle infinitively easier to endure.

All of my struggles moved me to recognize and embrace the following principle from my book *A*

Little Book of Big Principles—Values and Virtues for a More Successful Life: "It is from our greatest challenges that we often discover our true strengths."

1. Did you give-in to your struggles, or did you push yourself to get through and beyond them?

2. Did you blame someone else or anonymous others for your struggles and gave up, or did you instead focus on what you had to do to endure and eventually overcome them?

3. What have you learned about yourself from your struggles?

CHAPTER SEVEN

Solitude

"The best thinking has been done in solitude. The worst has been done in turmoil."

-- Thomas A. Edison

THE UNBELIEVABLE BLESSING OF SOLITUDE

The most revered religious and spiritual teachers of all time, at some point and very often, had their greatest moments of clarity and advancement during periods of solitude. It is in solitude that one is able to get in touch with their deepest internal desires and gain an understanding of who they are and what they exist to accomplish.

Solitude can be great fun, particularly for those with more introverted personalities. Solitude can also provide a benchmark for increasing one's contribution to society as a whole; within their own personal space, a person is allowed to explore and expand the thought processes of creativity and invent things that come from deep within the spirit, things that cannot be birthed without a deep and meaningful connection to one's own source of God-like power.

SOLITUDE AS A REGENERATOR OF ENERGY

In the current state of fast-paced living, the need for regeneration is strong and comes often. Being in a constant state of hustle and bustle and checking off one thing from our to-do list simply to move immediately on to another creates a living environment where the mind is constantly being activated and used to process external things. Spending so much time externally-focused on creating outer things can sometimes block the opportunity to play and enjoy life. Balance can be brought on by permitting oneself to delegate an equal amount of time to the focus of self. In this downtime, the soul can become re-energized for the tasks at hand, and the body can rest in preparation for the things to come.

Solitude also grants an escape from the judgment of the world. It is a safe-haven, and living within its walls, one finds comfort, peace, and the ability to grow. Without the judgment and opinion of others pressing in, a person is able to tap into their feelings and address those areas that call for attention and self-improvement.

The ability to take the time to look inside of self, and identify and correct areas of need opens us up to the potential to become our greatest, highest selves. A commitment to continually improvement may require much effort and an acceptance of the need for frequent change, but the outcome of feeling happier, more joyful, and stable in life is well-worth the quiet time spent.

"A man can be himself only so long as he is alone; and if he does not love solitude, he will not love freedom; for it is only when he is alone that he is really free."
- Arthur Schopenhauer, *Essays and Aphorisms*

THE FREEDOM FOUND IN SOLITUDE

In solitude there is also the freedom to create on a more artistic level. Writers, artists, designers, and storytellers are just a few professions that require a level of creativity that can only be found within the solitude of the mind. Breaking away from the chaos and congestion of daily living and tapping into the potential energy of life that propels us all and dictates the underlying causes for the majority of our decisions is something that is not easily done – and maybe even cannot be done - in a crowded room.

Alone, one is able to allow self-expression. The freedom to think thoughts that have never been thought; the freedom to speak words that have never been spoken; the freedom to build ideas that make no sense; and the freedom to transcribe dreams that have never been met. There is a freedom within solitude that allows us to take off the mask that we wear each day and instead be naked, bold, and transparent to ourselves. From this un-tethered height, the majority of the greatest ideas ever invented have sprung.

THE CONNECTION BETWEEN SOLITUDE AND PURPOSE

In such a vast space of creative liberty, it is impossible not to become more connected with oneself and one's Creator. Such freedom inspires boundless inventiveness and ushers in the abandonment of all fears, if we allow it to do so. Once free to think, feel, and simply be, the call of one's purpose is much more easily heard.

> "The greatest thing in the world
> is to know how to belong to oneself."
> - Michel de Montaigne, *The Complete Essays*

It is a call that reaches out to us more loudly during some parts of life than in others. The call and cry of our soul can walk us through this journey of life toward experiences that coincide with our personal meaning *of* life, and are the purposes *for* our being. The call is not loud; and the pull is not violent. It is found in the peace of solitude. There, we find our strength; in the quiet where outside voices are removed. In tranquility we can hear the direction and guidance of the heart, and follow the path unto which it guides us.

This inner guidance is always of great service to us. No matter what period of life we find ourselves undergoing at the moment, the guidance of the soul will always be there and will always be ready to help us when we ask. Solitude grants us the atmosphere required for the nurturing of these spiritual moments of clarity and preparation.

THE DANGERS OF SOLITUDE

Though glorious and helpful, solitude can sometimes have an adverse effect, depending upon the frame of mind of the person who is experiencing it.

For a person who feels emotions of loneliness, depression, or worry, solitude can further aggravate moods because there is nothing to create a contrasting perspective. If a person who is accustomed to having others to share their world with and go through tough times with finds himself alone and afraid, the results can be very damaging. They may not have the awareness that they are strong enough to deal with any situation that arises. In this attitude, a state of confusion and anger can develop, causing the situation to look worse than it is and induce feelings of helplessness that are difficult to overcome alone.

Solitude can also be taken to the extreme. There is a current rising in the discussion of introversion and people who seem to thrive on their own anti-social existence. Some say that many of the greatest computer programming geniuses and marketing innovators are introverts and are great at what they do because of it. The reasoning behind this notion is that the level of creativity and focus required to yield innovation in the areas of technology is something that comes about from one, simple, great idea— ideas that can only be born outside the presence of others.

There is a danger, however, in introversion-overload. People who become separated from day-to-day relationships, lose the benefit of connections and interactions. This is a problem because, at some point in every person's life, the need for another will arise. If we become too comfortable in our private sanctuaries, never emerging to find comfort nor clarity from other humans, the ability to form bonds with others can become increasingly elusive. As time progresses, it will become more difficult to initiate associations with others and even more difficult to build a rapport. This can have negative consequences emotionally, socially, professionally, and personally.

FINDING THE BALANCE

A balanced solitude-to-socialite equation will be different from person to person but must be addressed by those who tend to spend more than 70% of their time alone. Balance is essential in every area of life, and it's important to get outside of oneself and be inspired by the world. In it, there is much hope and opportunity. Outside of our walls and beyond the voices of our mind, we can find stimuli that encourages inventiveness and expands our vision of creativity. Getting outside of oneself also helps to ensure that we are constantly progressing in self-advancement. External occurrences can serve as pathways for originality and even be the spark of a genius revelation.

THE UNBELIEVABLE BLESSING OF SOLITUDE

Solitude does not mean loneliness, and being in the midst of many others does not automatically mean togetherness. I've been blessed to be able to spend many hours alone, but I seldom feel lonely.

Aloneness has allowed me to think clearly and deeply about things for which I had a concern and curiosity—hunger and poverty, outer space and ancient cultures.

One of my greatest passions is reading…I can sit and read for hours and not tire from it. I can become immersed in a book or work out lines of poetry and sentences for something I'm writing. In the blessing of solitude, I can "clear my head" or forget about all the minor inconveniences of life and become one with my thoughts, and in doing so, one with myself.

QUESTIONS TO THINK ABOUT....

1. Are you able to spend time alone without being lonely?

2. Can you find delight in sitting in complete silence while taking in all the glorious sounds of nature's beauty, splendor and, yes, silence?

CHAPTER EIGHT

Love

"One word frees us of all the weight and pain of life: That word is love."

-- Sophocles

THE UNBELIEVABLE BLESSING OF LOVE

Love is a blessing that has no single meaning. Not because it does not inspire enough words to compile a definition, but because, in defining it, so many words are simply left out. This is because love can have a very wide range of significance to different people. Not only this, but love can also have multiple meanings at different times to the very same person. Even further, there are also varying categories of love: there is romantic love, brotherly love, the love of a mother, the love identified by various religions and labeled as being the love of God; there is friendly love, and the love of one's craft; the love a person can feel for nature, self-love, and there is even love-hate.

Despite all of its types and definitions, the phrase "love" is one of the only words in the English language that consistently pulls up the same image in the mind and heart. Many terms have multiple meanings or can be taken in an ambiguous fashion, but, though it may be applied in different ways, only love is universal. Perhaps this is because it cuts to the core of the soul within all of us and touches who we are, even when we are trying to hide ourselves. Behind the masks that we wear, and beyond the image that we portray in front of others, true love can finally be found at the core of who we are.

Recognizing that at the core of us all lies tremendous love and beauty, it is slightly puzzling to consider why love is often credited with some of our greatest experiences of pain and disappointment. The following are some examples of how we use love in a negative fashion. Love is sometimes used as justification for decisions that may not otherwise have a leg upon which to stand. Love is often feared and avoided by those who have experienced it in the past. For these individuals, although love may have held many high points during its days of providing unspeakable pleasure, it ultimately crashed and burned in the end, leaving a painful memory.

Despite all our experiences with heartbreak and resolutions to shut ourselves off from the potential of a repeat experience, love remains and it is continually sought-after, and provides the fuel for our deepest passions and greatest achievements.

Where there is love there is life.
– Mahatma Gandhi

LOVE IS...

If you have ever read the single-image comic strip, "Love Is," penned by New Zealand's famous comic strip creator, Kim Grove, in the late 1960's, you will have brought into your mind many different answers for the question at hand. These quietly subtle and somehow perfectly-placed illustrations have informed readers around the globe of its perception of the meaning of love. Some of these statements have included, "love is, living for each other;" "love is, enjoying the simple things in life together;" "love is, not being put off by first appearances;" "love is, seeing him and everything." What many fans of this comic series do not know is that the creative quips originated as love notes the writer drew for her future husband. Although the author passed away in 1997, the legacy of love has lived on because of her three sons who continue to share with the world the meaning of love. [5]

The all-encompassing theme of this series is to sum-up the infinite meanings of love. Though many ideas are expressed, the premise always falls into one of a few categories: love is about the experiences you share with another; love is about the things you do and the actions you take in the name of caring for someone else; love is about the dialogue that you have within your mind regarding your own self-image; and love is about the moments we share and making it through life with someone else.

These underlying themes paint a picture of love that is about being both selfless and giving love, and also opening up to receive it. Yes, true love is both the giving and receiving of love and, for many of us, the receiving end is somehow the hardest part.

Being deeply loved by someone gives you strength, while loving someone deeply gives you courage.

– Lao Tzu

BEING OPEN TO RECEIVE LOVE

For every substance that exists, for every opportunity that presents itself, before action can be taken, receipt of the idea and agreement with seeing it come to pass must occur within one individual. We cannot experience something that we are not open to receive, and we cannot open up to something that we do not know is available. People often struggle with the idea of feeling as though they are worthy of receiving love. Often, these individuals did not grow up with parents who were overly affectionate or able to be very present in their lives for various reasons. If a person has not had the opportunity to grow up in a home where they were able to learn to receive love at an early age, it becomes something that must be practiced and specifically focused upon in order to expand one's capacity and open the heart to receive.

Opening up your heart and becoming vulnerable is a frightening situation, of course. In fact, some find being available for love so frightening that they would rather stick to solo evenings alone than risk stepping out into the world and possibly getting hurt (yet again). However, living in a shell is not something that human beings were created to do, nor is it something that a person can successfully manage for very long. At some point, the need to get out and spread one's wings becomes not only inevitable, but crucial to any mission for success. Being able to open up to love prior to arriving in situations where receiving love can improve circumstances will greatly increase the odds of performing satisfactorily when the moment has risen. In other words, practice always does make perfect and setting the scenery of your heart to prepare for the inception of love is the very best way for it to begin to be received.

One of the most unbelievable blessings of love is found in the way we forgive one another. Forgiveness is all about love because it requires the application of unconditional love, no matter which direction the forgiveness is flowing. If a person is offering forgiveness to another, it takes a decision to love no matter what the other person has done. When a person offers forgiveness to him or herself, unconditional love is being displayed in letting go of the need to feel grief and guilt for one's past actions. The fruit of love is born by forgiveness and brings with it the emotions of happiness, freedom, and joy.

The fruits of love can be recognized the world over, no matter what language a person may speak. Underneath the positive emotions brought on by love, whether it be romantic, friendly, or otherwise, a feeling of empowerment, fulfillment, and connection with the very essence of life is bound to sprout. These seeds of love are planted deep within the heart and can never be displaced. That is what makes love such a powerful thing, and its fruits so very poignant. Just as roses have an aroma that fills the air, so in fact does the glorious blessing of love have a fragrance that penetrates our surroundings with emotional bliss.

As giving love to others is so important for our own personal peace, receiving love directed towards oneself is also a critical aspect of a healthy state of being.

Self-love is the beginning of all other extensions of love. True love or pure love cannot come from a source that it does not already embody and, therefore, the love of oneself is truly paramount above all.

Loving oneself is a natural trait that is typically removed at a very young age by the conditioning of parenting that requires us to fulfill the needs of others in order to feel fulfilled within ourselves. Being a "good boy" requires the turning over of instinctive gratification in the name of following directions and doing as we are told. Although this teaching is not done with a malicious heart, its lasting effect must be overcome. This is because, in our upbringing, we have been conditioned to believe that we're not doing good things unless or until we are doing what someone else has outlined for us to do. The most debilitating effect of this mindset is that it keeps us from tapping into the passions of our hearts and living fully for ourselves from our own reservoir of desires and intents. If we were fully free to make our decisions without the background chatter of someone else's wishes, our lives would begin to take on a dynamic nature of their own whereby we would be able to realize the fulfillment of our life's purpose and experience joy beyond measure. Many people today, particularly in America, never reach this state of living in nirvana because we are not taught to overcome the barriers that have been put in place, and are keeping us from being able to fully accept ourselves. Without self-acceptance, we are removed from our ability to practice self-love and receive its unlimited benefits.

Just as the mind was untrained from the natural state of loving oneself, the mind can be retrained to look upon the self and self-desires with acceptance. Once the mind has been converted to its original self-loving state, the individual becomes free to enjoy the fullness of life, make mistakes and accept the consequences with grace and lightheartedness. Ultimately the person is now free to fully open up to the world and let their light so shine as to be felt by all who surround them. With this freedom comes power, and with that power comes innovation, and with the power to innovate the person can now change the world and cause it to become however they see fit.

THE UNBELIEVABLE BLESSING OF LOVE

We love others because we choose to, not because we have to, and we can't make anyone love us, no matter how much we might love them. In some instances, the more we love them, the less they tend to show love for us, or appreciate our presence. I have learned that if you love someone, it is best you do it unconditionally, but not blindly. You learn that you have the capacity to love again after being scorned. You realize that if someone cannot see and appreciate you for who you are and your devotion to them, they are doing you a favor by scorning you. They are demonstrating that they don't deserve your love! But the greatest blessing you will find in love comes when you grow to a place of maturity that allows you to have the capacity to love someone, even if they do not love you.

QUESTIONS TO THINK ABOUT....

1. Are you able to express your love and affection for all humanity?

2. Are you able to demonstrate your love and deep affection for the most important person in your life?

CHAPTER NINE

Helping Others

"If you want happiness for an hour, take a nap.

If you want happiness for a day, go fishing.

If you want happiness for a year, inherit a fortune.

If you want happiness for a lifetime, help somebody."

- **Chinese Proverb**

THE UNBELIEVABLE BLESSING OF HELPING OTHERS

As we become more mature in our lives, we begin to accept that life has a ying and yang balancing dimension to it. As important as it is to love oneself (critical, in fact), having a solely self-focused lifestyle is something that goes directly against our nature as human beings. Despite our animal instincts, we only find true pleasure in life when we feel that our own needs are being met while simultaneously meeting the needs of others.

It is understandable in this modern age of competition and ladder-climbing that many of us struggle to attain this balance. The problem is that, once one height of success is reached, we always have to go for the next. In that cyclical pattern, no relief can ever be found and no true joy can ever be experienced because we have no one with whom to share the victory of our success.

HOW IT FEELS TO HELP OTHERS SUCCEED

The feelings that come from helping others to realize their vision is almost indescribable. Even for a person with the most self-focused tendencies, when an opportunity to be of service to others arises, they cannot often resist accepting it. Even if they do, for whatever reason, choose to reject the opportunity, the thought of having done so typically sticks with them in the form of guilt for quite a while. This is because it is in our physical nature to give, do, and be of service to everyone we encounter, be it a friend, family member, or even a stranger. Our brains are equipped to find ways to naturally engage in fulfilling a purpose, and, when a chance presents itself to do so, no matter what it is, our natural inclination is toward being a help.

Assistance to others can be provided in a wide range of ways, from something as small as helping to run an errand or complete a task; to something as large as providing financial investments for startup entrepreneurs; to something as vital as providing assistance for someone who is physically incapable. The range of ways in which we can help one another is vast and possibly never-ending. These same words can be used to describe the feeling of happiness that we obtain within when we do so. There is great joy that stirs within our hearts when we see that something we have done has created a genuine difference in another person's life…it is somewhat indescribable. For some, these feelings of elation can even include the physical sensation of a tingling throughout the body. This means that, when helping others, our body has such a positive response toward providing value to others that our physical makeup changes and energy sparks and becomes more alive throughout our cells. Not many other things in life create such a physical reaction, so there must be something truly fantastic about the act of helping people and being of service to others.

FINDING STRENGTH IN THE COMMON GOAL

Reaching for our goals does require quite a bit of alone time and focus upon our objective. However, feeling self-sufficient and independent is sometimes confused with being a lone ranger. Some of our ambitions require skill sets and an investment of time that we, as individuals, cannot efficiently provide. In those cases, we require help from others in order to create our visions and successfully reach our destinations.

In addition to benefiting from the resources and capabilities of others, having people help in achieving the dream is also very empowering. When we share a common goal and a common intent, the power of that purpose is magnified tremendously, and our own internal energies are amplified by the presence of that external support. While learning not to rely entirely upon the support of others is very critical for long-term success and stability, in moments where we have the option for beneficial help, it is to be appreciated and embraced.

One of the greatest struggles of some ambitious people is in learning to open up to relationships and people in their lives and allowing themselves to receive the help of external resources that can help them attain the achievements they desire. Typically, this frame of mind comes from past experiences of hurt or of being let down by others, and it is the result of a decision, instead, to rely solely upon one's own mechanisms and resources in life. It is understandable that, after experiencing previous disappointments, a person would put up boundaries of protection in an attempt to deter repeat circumstances. However, at times we tend to build those walls a bit too high, which can result in us missing out on people and opportunities that we would, otherwise, find greatly beneficial.

It is very important to learn to leave those tendencies behind and face new possibilities with an open heart and a positive expectation. The easiest way to do so is to make a new decision that, even if it doesn't go according to plan, we are going to commit to the idea that everything will progress as we hope it will and encourage that thought with the action of opening up to prospects and possibilities that present themselves to us. Filtering through these options and listening closely to our hearts will help ensure that our most desired outcomes come about. No matter what, shedding the fear of being hurt and accepting help from others when necessary can provide a much higher potential for success.

Additionally, when we allow others to help us, we are actually providing a wonderful gift to them as well. As discussed earlier, the feelings that we have when we extend a hand to help others create a beautiful vibration of love that is essential to our human existence. When we allow others to feel the emotions that come with giving, we give them the opportunity to fulfill their own need to give to others, and we allow them to bring the light and love of that act into their own life experience and benefit from its presence. By accepting the help of others, we not only receive the gift of their help, but we also support their spiritual growth and happiness by allowing them the option. In that, we find that the blessing of giving to others is an infinite loop that serves both the giver and receiver and may very well be the greatest expression of true love that we can aspire to.

"The purpose of life is not to be happy. It is to be useful, to be honorable, to be compassionate, to have it make some difference that you have lived and lived well."

- Ralph Waldo Emerson

GETTING THE MOST OUT OF YOUR GIVING

It is generally accepted that sometimes people do things with ulterior motives in mind. It is also acknowledged that making the decision to help someone with the goal of receiving something in return almost never produces the results we really want. In addition to creating an unpredictable situation, doing things for the sole purpose of getting something in return also negates the nature of who we are and, thus, keeps us from receiving the benefits previously mentioned when we take the opportunity to give to others.

Therefore, when giving, be sure to do so with an open heart that has no thought for a return. This will serve both the giver and the recipient in many, many ways and is the very best way to be of genuine service to others.

GETTING IN A GIVING MOOD AND FINDING RECIPIENTS

All that is required to get into the mood for giving is the simple desire to do so. Giving is such an automatic component of who we are that acting upon this instinct requires no effort whatsoever; it is simply something that we do. Just as making the decision to be of help to others is an automatic, self-fulfilling intent, finding those in need can also be automatic. When we open up our hearts to be of service, many beautiful things can happen, one of which being that those who are in need of what we have to offer begin naturally showing up in our lives. It is a bit like asking a question and then noticing that, without even trying, the answer shows up for you. Just in that manner, when we decide to place our attention toward helping others and giving to them, something within our spirits causes us to magnetize ourselves to one another and easily find a recipient for our compassionate state of love.

THE UNBELIEVABLE BLESSING OF HELPING OTHERS

I have been blessed to have a family, particularly my totally devoted mother, who daily demonstrated examples of helping others. This wonderful blessing was passed on to all ten siblings (Yes, there are actually ten of us!) who choose to consistently help others in many different ways. We grew up unafraid to share our time, talents and treasure to help those in need and, to this day, we continue to share with others and contribute to communal efforts.

I have learned that, no matter what you have, there's something you have to offer the world and something you have that will be of benefit to others. In my family, we were able to share vegetables from the garden, and farm-raised meats from slaughtered animals. We shared farming chores, and participated with other families in the exchange of assistance.

There are opportunities everywhere to be a blessing to others: people needing somewhere to live or transportation, people in need of education, and even those simply in need of some guidance. Whatever you choose to do to help others, the most important thing is that you enjoy helping those who are in need. I have also learned that, when helping others, it is crucial to remember to also tend to the progression of your own life and ambitions. The reason for this is that the more you learn the more you can earn; and the more you earn, the better position you are in to help others.

1. What can you do to lighten the burden of someone in obvious need?

2. Can you see beyond your circumstance and recognize that there is someone much less fortunate and could use your assistance, including offering encouragement, inspiration and motivation?

3. In some small way, how can you enrich the life of someone less fortunate than you?

CHAPTER TEN

Opportunity

"Opportunity is missed by most people because it is dressed in overalls and looks like work."

-- Thomas A. Edison

THE UNBELIEVABLE BLESSING OF OPPORTUNITY

Oh, the possibilities that life envelops for each and every one of us if we only knew that they were there! It is the blessing of opportunity that pulls toward us all of the wonderful blessings in life and joins us together in one beautifully orchestrated composition that we call "life."

Every single blessing that life has to offer points to the creation of an opportunity. Your choice of desired opportunities can be absolutely anything you desire; have a particular experience or go to a particular place; have a relationship that has certain characteristics; create something or make a dream become a reality. Opportunities are around us and draw to us even more opportunities for expression, expansion and the fulfillment of cherished goals.

The race is not to the swift or the battle to the strong,
nor does food come to the wise or wealth to the brilliant or
favor to the learned; but time and chance happen to them all.
- Ecclesiastes 9:11

There is an opportunity in the blessing of time. Time is the ultimate opportunity because it is the very thing that creates the likelihood of all our options. Within time, opportunities to change our circumstances, shift our focus, or embrace something new all exist, and they exist simultaneously. At any given moment in time, you have the opportunity to jump from one decision to the next or to create one experience or another. This is a phenomenon that we rarely give enough attention and value to. What it means is that because of the opportunity time allots, at any given moment you have the ability to make choices and take actions that can entirely change the trajectory of the life you are now experiencing. It doesn't matter what it is you are aspiring to create, whether it be something positive, or negative, or something that simply "just is"; the blessing of opportunity provides you with the capability of changing absolutely anything you desire by utilizing the blessing of time to make focused and clear decisions.

"Teachers open the doors, but you must enter yourself."
- Chinese Proverb

There is opportunity in the blessing of religious freedom. Religious freedom grants us the wide open spaces to do whatever we feel is important to us as individuals and valuable within our lives. The necessity for religious freedom grants our leaders and governments the opportunity to respectfully fulfill their role to citizens and provide a protection that allows each one of us to cultivate and expand who we are as we each see fit. This allows an unending number of opportunities to be generated in our personal and private realm, giving us the power to turn each of our visions, no matter how wild or outside of the box, into something we are able to experience, embrace, and share with the world. This is the greatest opportunity possible for freedom of expression.

There is an opportunity in the blessing of family. Drawing near to others and drawing them near to you, whether they are a blood relative or very close friend, can create a sense of stability in a person's life, allowing them to stand tall and firm in their beliefs and determination. Family can provide the strength and support necessary to take flight toward ambitious goals. Even if their support is not demonstrated in a positive manner, the presence of other people in your life can motivate you because they are helping you to succeed. It can motivate you to show others the expanse of your skills and capabilities; or it can motivate you by providing you with work to do that fulfills a purpose or empowers the life of someone you love.

There is an opportunity in the blessing of good health. This blessing is one that simply cannot be overlooked and provides you with a strong foundation for success. With a healthy body and a healthy mind, there are very few things that you cannot accomplish. This state of physical well-being is a blessing because it allows you to take hold of every opportunity that comes forth. Good health often goes unnoticed and un-thanked, so be sure to notice it, and thank it, and be very happy for it. Use it to the best of your abilities by fully grabbing hold of the opportunities that present themselves in your life.

"Opportunities are on every hand; what we need is, not a new chance, but clearness of vision to discern the chance which at this very hour is ours, if we recognize it."
- Katherine Krieger

There is opportunity in the blessing of single parenting. Being a single parent allows you to have the opportunity to really see what you are made of. You will face situations where you have to make decisions that result in you defining who you are not because the decisions are so difficult or so bad, but because in order to make some decisions in life, you have to draw a line in the sand and that line becomes a part of the meaning of who you are.

In the middle of difficulty lies opportunity.
- Albert Einstein

There is opportunity in the blessing of struggle. The struggle in this is the opportunity to see what we are truly made of and to grow from that inner knowing. Struggle allows us to practice changing the ways in which we define things that occur in our lives and try to approach them from a different perspective. It presents challenges to keep us on our toes and constantly striving for something more. Struggle is the transitional state that brings about some of our greatest opportunities.

The opportunity found in solitude grants us space for feelings of peace and reinvigoration. Solitude allows springs of creativity to burst forth, allowing us to obtain the energy and fuel required in order to paint our greatest masterpieces in life. This opportunity provides us with the grounding we need in order to remain centered while surrounded by all the hustle and bustle of daily life. Solitude helps us to equip ourselves in the dark for successfully navigating the vast array of possibilities and promises available in the light.

Love is the opportunity to truly be alive. Its blessings are numerous and span the far reaches of time. Love builds us up and binds all things to a never-ending source of vibrant potential. There are opportunities to find and feel love; there are opportunities to share in the spread of love. However, you find it and in whatever way it is transmitted, the opportunity for love is ever-present and always fulfilling its purpose.

"A pessimist sees the difficulty in every opportunity; an optimist sees the opportunity in every difficulty."
- Winston Churchill

The greatest opportunity that can be found in helping others is in the connecting of oneself to the possibility of serving a greater good. Helping others feeds the soul and quiets the mind; it relaxes the muscles and softens the heart; it gives us a reason for being. Helping others is an act that transfers positive energy in both directions: to the recipient and to the giver. Its life-giving nature is the driving force deep within us all and provides us with the opportunity to feel of value to others and to fulfill our glorious purpose.

"The golden moments in the stream of life rush past us, and we see nothing but sand; the angels come to visit us, and we only know them when they are gone."
- George Eliot

THE UNBELIEVABLE BLESSING OF OPPORTUNITY

Millions of people around the world have not had a fraction of the opportunities we often take for granted. Nearly each and every person reading this text has been blessed with the opportunity to: go to school, pursue their passion, and to live and move about in relative safety.

Opportunities to aspire to do or become whatever I wanted to do with my life have been ever-present and always unfolding. The crux was not in the availability of opportunity but in the need to discover the truth that it was always up to me to decide what I wanted to do with those opportunities, whether they were limited or unlimited. I clearly realized that it was not going to be easy and, most importantly, I acknowledged that I did not have to secure anybody's permission in order to succeed.

The thing that has created the greatest difference in my life was having the ability to see and seize those opportunities, and the conviction to make the decision and commitment to do so.

"Yesterday is gone. Tomorrow has not yet come. We have only today. Let us begin." - Mother Teresa

QUESTIONS TO THINK ABOUT....

1. What have you done with the opportunities you have had or have been given?

2. Did you make the most of opportunities you have had, or did you do just enough to say you did something with them?

3. What have you done to help others to see opportunities waiting to be taken advantage of?

4. What have you done to give others opportunities to "shine" or show what they can do?

5. Do you see challenges as insurmountable obstacles or as opportunities to be seized?

Personal Reflections...

ABOUT THE AUTHOR

Dr. Wil Brower is an educator, professional facilitator, lecturer, mediator, and writer. His books are adaptations of the wisdom he has accrued from his varied life experiences, which range from the United States Air Force veteran, corporate executive and Business Education and English/Language Arts teacher.

Having gained his practical knowledge for success from his vast amount of experience and affiliations, Dr. Brower has worked with organizations such as Hewlett-Packard Corporation, Marriott Corporation, The University of Memphis, DuPont Pharmaceuticals, Dow Chemical Company, U.S. Veterans Administration, the State of Arkansas, Raleigh News and Observer, the U.S. Army Corps of Engineers, and the U.S. Postal Service. He is also the Founder of the non-profit organization, Institute for Youth Development and Educational Resources, Inc. (IYDER).

Dr. Brower, a U. S. Air Force veteran and former executive with Bell Telephone Laboratories and AT&T, is also the author of A Little Book of Big Principles—Values and Virtues for a More Successful Life (1998); Me, Teacher, Me...Please!--Observations about Parents, Students and Teachers and the Teacher-Learning Process (2002); English Grammar and Writing Made Easy—Learn how to express yourself more accurately, concisely and clearly with a few easy lessons (2009); Traffic Signs on the Road of Life (2012; When Justice Calls—A Novel (2013); Seven C's of Success—Developing the Attributes, Attitudes and Behaviors to Achieve All You Want Out of Life (2013); and What a Difference a Comma Makes-- (2016).

Additionally, some of his writings on the subjects of human and organizational development and personal effectiveness have appeared in Harvard Business Review (1996) and Cultural Diversity at Work (1997). For more information or to request Dr. Brower attending your event as a speaker, please email wlbrower@gmail.com.

CITATIONS

1

International Religious Freedom Act Information

http://www.state.gov/j/drl/rls/fs/2011/170637.htm

2

First Amendment Rights

http://www.forwardprogressives.com/explaining-freedom-of-religion-for-those-who-seem-unable-to-understand-what-it-means/

3

Glory of OM: A Journey to Self-Realization

http://www.goodreads.com/work/quotes/43148878

http://www.goodreads.com/author/show/4123171.Banani_Ray

4

Kim Grove, "Love Is," New Zealand's famous comic strip creator

http://www.myperfectline.com/2012/09/50-cute-love-is-comics-by-kim-casali.html

Made in the USA
Columbia, SC
28 February 2025

54531785R00061